Dudley's Undoubtedly Useful Products

A Compendium of Highlights from John Dudley & Co's
Legendary Mail Order Catalogue
1914–1931

•

Compiled by Mark Luiggi

Dudley's Undoubtedly Useful Products
A Compendium of Highlights from John Dudley & Co's
Legendary Mail Order Catalogue, 1914–1931

ISBN: 978-1-63381-048-8

My sincere thanks to Christine Luiggi for her design skills in assembling this book. A special thanks to Joe Ofria whose skills with Photoshop have been invaluable to this project, as well as many others, over the last ten years. Thanks Joe! Also thanks to Kathryn Liebowitz for copyediting and proofreading.

Dangerous Trick Press • 1165 Massachusetts Avenue, Arlington MA 02476

Produced by
Maine Authors Publishing, Rockland, Maine
www.maineauthorspublishing.com

Printed in the U.S.A.

Foreword

In September 1996, while stumbling around in a dark attic at an estate sale being conducted at a private home in Ipswich, Massachusetts, I came upon a dusty wooden box that had the barely legible label "Dudley & Co, Chicago" pasted at an angle across its top. With anticipation I quickly pried off the loosely nailed boards to reveal what looked to be a collection of *Dudley's Undoubtedly Useful Products*, the famous and rare mail order catalogues widely coveted by antiquarians. In my giddy surprise at this remarkable discovery, I straightened up sharply only to have my head meet a low-running ceiling beam with some force. After a brief period of unconsciousness I regained my composure and somewhat unsteadily set about examining in detail exactly what I had found. Ranging from the years 1915 to 1927, it appeared to be a nearly complete set of the catalogues that occupy a unique niche in the history of American retailing. I resolved to make it my mission to share my discovery, and what follows here are highlights gleaned from these rare and precious volumes.

—Mark Luiggi, 2015

Introduction

It may seem hard to imagine, but there was a time when having a Really Big Machine purring away in your front parlor was a mark of status and family pride much coveted by America's newly rising middle class. It would have been difficult to find a home of the era that didn't have at least one pair of Pedestal Leg Rests or to find a child who wouldn't be thrilled at the prospect of an exciting session with the Block o' Wood Plaything. Grandfather probably painted his barn and every other knickknack around the house with the devastatingly effective Color Cannon, while many grandmothers were known to rely extensively on the clockwork-driven La-La-Bye Wagon as a practical and economical way to help care for young children. These and many other products all sprang from the lively imagination of John Dudley, a man who was destined to reshape the burgeoning mail order business of the early 20th century with his unique—some would say quirky—vision.

As the son of a successful purveyor of unconventional agricultural implements, Dudley was introduced at a young age to the hurly-burly world of retailing as it existed in the latter part of the19th century. Starting off by selling bits of string and small rocks from the back of a horse cart, he quickly built a reputation as a salesman of prodigious ability. As his business and confidence grew, he settled into a storefront location on Chicago's south side, where he quickly came to the realization that mail order companies, such as Montgomery Ward and Sears, Roebuck & Company, were the way of the future. In an effort to distinguish himself from these giants he determined to present a range of goods that would go far beyond what they were purveying. If Montgomery Ward offered a set of chairs, Dudley would offer a complete set of chairs; if Sears, Roebuck & Company offered a bicycle, Dudley would offer a magic bicycle. With an eye to the public's fascination with gadgetry and a finger on their occasional gullibility, Dudley craftily carved out a sizable niche in the imagination of the American public, and they loved him for it. Crowds lined up, cheerfully parting with money in anticipation of the fulfillment these marvelous goods would surely bring.

The following pages contain a small sample of the hundreds of products invented by Dudley & Co's legendary research and development team during the golden years of 1915–1927. Categories such as "Properly Sized Home Furnishings," "Splendid Devices of Several Types," and "Extraordinarily Personal Products" give us some idea of the surprising range of Dudley's ingenuity.

Baby's First Walker

This modern adjustable walker allows baby to learn to walk at an adult height. It eliminates baby's feeling of insignificance often experienced in old-fashioned walkers. Eye-to-eye contact with adults establishes positive self-esteem and generally improves baby's psychological outlook. Free-rolling casters and all hardwood construction ensure a lifetime of utility.

BHL 73 903 . . . . $5.35

Really Big Machine

By Jove! It will take up an immense portion of your drawing room, but there's no denying that this is a machine to be reckoned with. Impressive, yet simple and effective, it represents the pinnacle of modern achievement and is a marked improvement over the common Big Machine. Electrical lights, a fine mahogany finish, and heavy nickel plating all combine to convey an overwhelming display of usefulness. From the moment its serene hum and purposeful clicking begin you can rest assured that it will be capable of completing a myriad of tasks in the home and at the factory. A splendid value at twice the cost.

WTG 75 342 . . . . $27.23

Life Saving Device For Persons Not Wishing To Raise Their Voice In An Unseemly Manner

Whether you've fallen off a ferry or have been dragged out to sea in an undertow, there's no need to worry if you've remembered to bring this clever device! Simply engage the mechanism and a discreet "Help" will emanate from the amply proportioned sound trumpet. Having been thus alerted, the proper authorities will speedily come to your rescue, and you will not have had to resort to shouting, arm waving, or other foolish-looking behavior.

HJC 43 805 . . . . $11.63

Pedestal Leg Rests

As used for many years by health-conscious Europeans, these doctor-approved pedestals provide a natural way of restoring circulation to tired legs, sharpen your mental acuity, and generally improve your sense of balance. Pedestals are of sturdy oak construction topped with a comfy velvet cushion and are available in two sizes depending on the degree of reinvigoration that you require. One would be equally comfortable using these attractively designed devices in the home, at the club, or while traveling by public transportation.

BB A 6 354. . . . . $2.10

Single Octave Piano

A godsend to those of a musical persuasion who are compelled to hold a tight rein on their purchases. Each fully functional and richly toned instrument comprises one full octave of thirteen white and black keys. As your financial and musical abilities increase, you may add successive octaves to eventually create a whole piano. Take a few octaves on a camping trip; lend an octave to a friend! The many advantages of this clever design will readily become apparent.

PGF 08 088 . . . .$4.45

Big Wig

If your natural ambition inclines you toward running large civic projects, arranging massive loans for titans of industry, or simply having breakfast with the president you'll appreciate the value of our Big Wig. Stylish yet understated, this 100% llama hair wig will mark you as a man of gravity and substance. Specify style: Sovereign, Colossus, or the ever popular Autocrat.

KYE 72 453 . . . . $3.43

Magic Bicycles

These are the kind of bicycles every boy and girl really wants. After learning a few easily remembered magic words your child will soon be doing the kind of tricks that would make a circus performer quit the circus and head for the hills! Dematerialize yourself and go through walls without a scratch! Become invisible! Go forward and backward in time! Fly over tree tops! Yes, these bikes do it all and yet never need repairs of any kind. They're magic!

HTY 89 345 . . . . $14.93

Home-Twice-As-Big Goggles

Why move to a larger house when for a surprisingly affordable price you can make your existing home appear twice as big as it really is? Give your cozy and perhaps somewhat cramped quarters a more palatial aspect! Save on moving and finance charges! Cancel that major renovation! The attractive rubber goggles are so comfortable that you'll soon forget you're even wearing them. Buy extra sets so your guests and pets can enjoy your newly spacious surroundings too!

773 4 HSP . . . . $2.56 each

Block O' Wood Plaything

This is a toy that stimulates rousing good fun among persons vigorous enough to tolerate a great deal of excitement. Wholesome games like "Stop! Don't Go!" "Lie There," and the subtly suspenseful "Absolutely Still!" have been thrilling partygoers for generations. This finely finished block of mahogany will give many years of trouble-free activity and will require a minimum of care and attention. Don't let your next party be dull and dreary...get a Block o' Wood Plaything and let the good times "Stop!"

GSR 7 320 . . . .$1.03

Burst-Into-Flame Alarm Clock

Put the "alarm" back into "alarm clock" with this modern alternative to the old-fashioned, easily ignored, tinkling bell type of clock. Bursting into flame at the hour you predetermine, it will demand your immediate attention and will have you wide awake in an instant. A handy fire extinguisher may be ordered separately, and a direct line to your local fire department is recommended. A thoughtful gift for the difficult to rouse.

BB A 6 354 . . . .$2.10

Bi-Scopic Phonograph Set

This set occasionally creates a startlingly realistic "Bi-Scopic" sound by utilizing two phonographs playing the same record in precise synchrony. No complicated mechanism to foul up or run afoul of. One simply starts the first phonograph and then quickly runs over to the second phonograph to start it. Settling back into your favorite chair you may, from time to time, enjoy the thrilling "Bi-Scopic" sound that puts you right into the center of the orchestra!" "Devilishly difficult to synchronize but well worth the effort," says one well-known music critic. A wonderful way to double the cost of your record collection!

PGR 22 369 . . . . $8.22

Clock Tower in Your Yard

Erect a full-scale clock tower in your yard. Tower stands 150 feet high and sports a thirty-foot-diameter clock on each façade, which may be read from anywhere in your neighborhood. A friendly, impressive way to say, "Howdy, neighbor!" Specify St. Michael's or Westminster chimes.

PQR 63 932 . . . . $1,123.56

Modern Kitchen Set

Free yourself from kitchen drudgery with this up-to-the-minute set, which has finally been perfected after years of study and experimentation. This modern motorized kitchen facilitates all aspects of sanitary food preparation and requires absolutely no watching. Substantially made of solid oak and cast iron, this set will propel you and your family into a future you have scarcely dared dream of. Cast-iron wheels will not mar floors. Free extra set of dishes provided.

773 4 HSP . . . . $2.56 each

Set of Trained Birds

This set of highly trained birds will become an integral component in the successful management of your home. They will assist in the preparation of children's meals, make minor repairs to radio equipment, and even rearrange your schedule to allow more time to devote to business matters. Never rude or unruly, these French-speaking birds will create just the right impression in their smart uniforms and caps.

HSP 32 938 . . . . $7.48

Complete Set of Chairs

Whether entertaining foreign dignitaries or just the old gang, why be caught in the potentially awkward situation of not having the precisely correct size chair on hand? With a set like this you will be able to effortlessly match each guest to a suitable, sensible chair and thus eliminate needless squabbling and the potential legal difficulties such mismatches may provoke. Far superior to the incomplete set often found at other mail order establishments seeking to hoodwink an unsuspecting public.

HL 89 947 . . . . set of six $8.56

Great Monument To Yourself

Haven't accomplished anything truly noteworthy? Not likely to? Instead of dwelling on it in an unseemly display of self-pity, why not immerse yourself in a major construction project that will ensure the memory of your somewhat unremarkable life? Using proven Roman construction techniques, these marble-clad concrete structures will be around for a long, long time with your name engraved right on the front! Handy "temples" provide excellent storage space for lawn furniture, etc. Please inquire about optional eternal flame.

BTX 45 343 . . . . . $1602.79

Painting With A Rude Message

For those occasions when it is difficult to reveal your true feelings to a business associate or relative, why not communicate through the elevating medium of art? Using real oil paints on canvas, our professional artist will cleverly conceal your rude and insulting remark in an otherwise charming landscape. We will take care of all matters pertaining to the delivery of the painting, and you will take continuing pleasure in the knowledge that so beautiful a gift will be hung in a prominent place in the recipient's home.

CGH 3 760. . . . . $2.01

La-La Bye Wagon With Mechanical Horse

An ideal combination which has been the choice of thousands of mothers. This prancing mechanical horse with glass eyes is hitched to a gaily colored metal wagon. A safe and pleasant place for baby while the busy mother attends to her housework and other chores. Will take place of a nurse girl in many homes.

HKT 42 756 . . . . $1.68

Miniature Dogs

Tiny but hearty, these exceedingly small dogs will allow families previously unable to afford canine companionship to join the happy ranks of contented dog owners without the fuss and expense of larger breeds. These lively, clear-eyed dogs have velvety coats, sweet tiny barks, and are bubbling over with vim. They will enthusiastically retrieve small objects from beneath heavy furniture and herd unwanted insects out of the house and are proven to be surprisingly effective against burglars. Weighing a scant one quarter-pound, they will save their thrifty owner a fortune in dog food. So small you'll want to own a bunch!

BB A 6 354 . . . . $2.56 each

Print Your Own Novel

Enables you to print a professional looking book right in your own home. Self-inking hand-operated press with movable rubber type will produce a real book that will be salable in bookstores from coast to coast. Easy-to-follow instructions show you how to create fascinating stories with compelling characters that will undoubtedly captivate the attention of a wide reading public and launch you on the well-compensated literary career that you've been dreaming of. Press stands 14 inches tall and is nicely painted.

CLT 3 540 . . . . $6.33

Color Cannon

Why be encumbered by unpleasant, messy painting chores when a few quick blasts from this industrial-strength apparatus will make short work of even the largest projects you care to undertake? Throw away antiquated brushes, rollers, and even ladders, because now you can cover everything as far as the eye can see with a thick, labor-saving coat of durable paint. A barn, a bridge, or a table top can all be completed in a blinding flash without even having to remove your coat and hat!

WXR 40 354 . . . . $26.30

Portable Reference Library

A novel solution to the formerly unrecognized problem of not having a well-rounded reference library at your fingertips at all times. Whether your travels take you to the heart of a busy city or to a sunny seaside resort, you will never again be unable to answer the many questions that are bound to present themselves to the modern family. This fine set of encyclopedias and dictionaries, together with a number of specialized volumes such as *Motorcar Mechanics*, *Anecdotes of the Great War*, and *How to Box*, will always be at the ready to help you settle arguments, identify rare birds, fix clocks...the answers are all here when you need them!

BN 4 839 . . . . $8.56

"Double Dog" Eight Wheel Bike

With a bark and a yip to announce its arrival, children and parents alike will delight in this practical vehicle. Perfect for the child who may be too small to pedal or balance a regular bicycle, and it runs on inexpensive dog pellets! Extra motivation for your capable canines is provided by tantalizing genuine beefy-aroma dog bones hanging just out of their eager reach. Easily-attachable leather harnesses will accommodate varying sizes of dogs, although "toy" breeds are not recommended.

PLQ 62 458 . . . . $6.12

88 Key Piano

Teaches the first principles of music. Your child will be overjoyed at the dainty tone of this instrument. Wood case has rosewood finish, hinged cover, and a paneled front. A suitable piano for a small child.

HGE 70 803 . . . . $2.75

Bouncing Balls

Inquisitive minds will expand as they contemplate the mystery of these fascinating bouncing balls. Without the aid of wires, strings, or a motor of any kind, these balls, when dropped, will eerily bounce back as if by magic. Balls may also be rolled.

HTY 42 756 . . . .$1.68

Live-In Real Life Strong Man

Why kick yourself when this burly fellow can do it for you? Drawn from the ranks of former circus performers, one of these very strong men will live in your home and always be at the ready to provide the discipline, backbone, and fortitude that you probably lack. Have him force you to quit smoking, cut down on alcohol, or desist from whatever untoward habits you may indulge in. "Being cuffed repeatedly on the ear really helped me to get on the right track!" says one happy subscriber. These strongmen will also prove useful in executing household tasks that require a great deal of strength. Strongman is English-speaking and never rude.

RLS 82 111 . . . .$23.41

Complete Waste of Time

If you're keen on frittering away the hours, you won't go wrong in choosing this unique item. Widely advertised in Finland and recommended by knowledgeable persons everywhere, it boasts these remarkable features: It is colorfully painted and has a small bell, and, although it seems to radiate an aura of delight, it will soon become apparent that, just as it says on the box, this device is a complete waste of time. In order to waste as much time as possible the Complete Waste of Time comes with a 276-page booklet that puts a myriad of time-wasting strategies at your fingertips and includes the surprisingly engaging story about how this extraordinary gadget has wasted time for generations of fun seekers.

SSR 7 124 . . . . $1.05

Artists' Studio Wear

These heavyweight cotton canvas suits will prove the perfect choice for artists who face the common anxiety of finding practical yet stylish clothing to wear in the studio. Conforming to internationally accepted standards of health and safety, these garments incorporate comfortable, unobtrusive rubber splash guards at the neck and wrists and provide protection from a myriad of media. Loose-fitting, attractive tailoring permits free movement of the arms and legs and is sure to encourage creative gestures of all types. High quality binocular–style eyewear will magnify and clarify your artistic vision!

BHL 73 903 . . . . $7.49

Giant Bunny

Finally a Giant Bunny where and when you need it! Whether it's an important business meeting, a cocktail party, or an intimate family gathering, this lovely 18-foot stuffed bunny will be the perfect accompaniment to your activities no matter how unusual. A conversation piece, a companion to the elderly, and an unequivocal testament to your sound judgment and good taste. This heirloom-quality bunny will impart a sense of grandeur and dignity to your next social event not easily achieved with lesser bunnies.

HKT 42 756 . . . . $16.68

Never-Lose Bookmark

The Never-Lose Bookmark effortlessly conquers the dedicated reader's constant concern—a lost bookmark. Based on certain theories of size and proportion not yet fully understood, the Never-Lose Bookmark will bring you the peace of mind that comes from having your bookmark in sight and at hand at all times. Fabricated in Honduras of fine leatherette, this product has been hailed as a splendid achievement by the reading public and others.

RTZ 4 367. . . . . $2.01